Brothers, Sisters, and Sinner Friends

Margie Ann Wright

Presentation by *BookLeaf Publishing*

Web: www.bookleafpub.com

E-mail: info@bookleafpub.com

ISBN: 9789358312195

First edition 2023

For Sharon, who took my sailor dress in exchange for a lifetime of joy. She has always, and forever, been my boon companion and greatest friend.

ACKNOWLEDGEMENT

I'd like to thank my brother, Ponder, who is Batman to my Robin, and taught me there is no gain without pain, and when the going gets tough, the tough get going. No guts, no glory. He taught me to crawl and then walk and eventually to tie a towel around my neck and fly! He instilled in me a certain love of life that even cancer could not quench. He is where I get my tenacity of hope.

A special shout out to Debbie, Sharon, Cheryl and Mrs. Dortha Shirley who have put up with all my Oxford Madness and now serve as the review committee for every thing I produce.

PREFACE

This anthology caught me in a time of struggle. My Oxford training has taught me that in my deepest struggle lies my greatest potential. In this book of both traditional poetry and prose poetry, I let my pen flow without a sensor and explore the gains amid the losses experienced not only by myself but also those of my mother and friends both old and new. There are celebrations of love and friendship as well as gratitude for the blessings of the past. Through it all that tenacity of hope shines through. These are my rainbows through the rain.

Oil and Ink

Somewhere between the pages of a thousand books and their daughter's typing, he lingers, waiting for her to come to him like she did in 1949.

She left Abilene with her roommate to go to a small school in Arkansas that promised enchantment of a different kind. Something new to her but that she understood when she first read the letters he had written his other girl friend, her roommate there in Texas, and she had started writing him back, pretending to be someone else and signing a name not her own.

Lingering in the back rooms, in belted trousers and his honest cotton shirt, he itches to pull a book out of the shelves of his library only three rooms deep because they moved so many times once they had kids, it was either leave books behind or leave the kids. He could never leave the kids not since the day Harvard had asked him to choose between being daddy or a scholar. It had been easy to quit Harvard before he had even taught his first class. You don't ask a real man stupid questions like that. So now, he just

has three rooms to haunt while he lingers
waiting on the queen of his heart to finish her
journey.

 Nothing of him remains except parchment and
Indian ink lingering between the lines. The
books camouflage him when she comes walking
into the library like it's 1949 when he caught her
reflection in the plate glass door and winked.

She is lost and wanders in to select a book. He
laughs out loud, because until he went to meet
his maker, she had never opened a book not even
the ones he had written. Books were her rival
and she had known it. Before his lips had ever
kissed hers, she had bought him a book. His first
book. He had spent his only plow-boy dime on a
coke for her, and she returned the gesture on his
birthday with a book she'd seen him fondling in
the bookstore when she was working the soda
fountain next door. She had taken her daddy's
oil-field-dollars and bought the book, though
they were "just Buddies."

His dime was worth more than a daddy-dollar
the minute she laid eyes on him. So much so,
that she was sure if she played her dominoes
right, she'd be giving up that Cadillac Daddy had
always promised to give her if she finished a

degree before she got a wedding ring. She would
be wearing that ring on her finger when they
handed her a diploma. So when she saw him
fondling the book, she realized, right then and
there, her life was going to be nothing like it
had been in the oil field. Nothing like his had
been in the farm fields. Their lives were going to
be of books and people and camaraderie,
because she wanted to be fondled just like that
book, and she wanted to always be worthy of his
last dime.

Still, she felt an odd resentment to the books,
because she knew he would go to them like
another mistress. He would leave her bed when
she slept and go to his book, whatever book he
owned. She couldn't cook yet, but she would
always be sure he had books and lots of them.
When her daddy had brought in the first oil
fields in Texas, he hadn't known it, but it had all
been a part of God's plan to get this delicious
farm boy a house full of children and books. Her
Buddy was proud and would never be bought, or
even accept her daddy's money, but she knew
that she could walk through his world of dimes
without a net because she had the safety of being
born in an oil field where you planted a dime
and it bloomed in fives and tens and twenties.
Her own daddy wanted her to be a college girl

because he had secretly wanted to but never had
the chance, so as much as he would hate the
Arkansas lad's dimes, he would salivate when he
saw the books lining the walls of what would be
his daughter's home.

 She wanders into the library, now, lingering,
even though her eyes are growing too tired to
read. She grins remembering how her daddy had
complained, in what secretly were actual brags
to his friends. His daughter had married a
professor with stripes down his sleeves and
books all over walls.

"He doesn't know how to eat a steak and wastes
his time and money on books."

He griped that they lived on campus and not in a
big house like his daughter and grandchildren
deserved. It was hard to sleep when he went to
visit because the typewriter sang all night.

" If the hay-bailer my daughter married isn't
reading a book, he is writing one, or teaching
idiots how to write one, or something like that.
And their boy has to sleep on the couch, because
the room that should have been a guest room is
an office. Whoever heard of an office in a

house? Why didn't he just have one at work like a normal guy?"

 She giggles, old and raspy now, but full of delighted cackles as she relives the day her daddy put in an office for himself at his and Momma's house and got some books and even a phone on the desk. Momma showed the neighbors, and Daddy secretly started school correspondence courses. He took to camouflaging it from everyone with miniature oil wells, rigs, and hard hats on book shelves and the furniture of his "oil man's office." He hung company photos on the walls. Oddly, enough, her Daddy's office wound up looking a lot like her lover's office.

She grows silent and a tear shimmers down her cheek as she recalls Daddy and how he had cried when her plow-boy walked across the stage and received his masters degree. It was the only time he let on how proud he was, although her Momma couldn't have a conversation without dropping hints about her son-in-law, the scholar, and what all he was up to. That was why, just before her love fell ill, Daddy had left her the farm. Momma had been so proud of the plow-boy's morals, work ethics, and rise to prominence as a scholar, that she had insisted

Daddy not sell the farm. On her death bed, she made Daddy vow to one day deed her the farm so they would be able to finally own a home. They were each pushing 60 by the time they designed and moved into their house with its rooms of books.

He lingers behind the chair feeling her feels, wiping her tears, but waiting for her to open the book so he can see the page. She stops to wipe tear and for a moment their fingers intertwine like they did in college whenever it rained. It begins to rain in his heart and he feels it twist and tighten in his chest as he reaches to hold her crinkled hand. She had always held his hand, storm or gentle shower, every time rain fell in their lives.

Ink falls in drops leaking from the edges of his heart as more of her tears flow. He tries to change the mood.

"Just remember I was the one who bought you the Cadillac even if it was used," he calls in a raised voice hoping this time she will hear.

Suddenly, she speaks, " Yes, and you waited until Daddy had passed away to keep from

hurting his pride. You always were respectful of
him even when he brayed like a mule."

The Indian ink stops in its tracks as his
parchment heart holds its breath. Can she hear
him? Does she know he Is here?

" Oh, love, it's time for me to go interrupt your
daughter and make her watch The Word Game
with me. If I don't, she'll type all night. You
would be so proud of her Oxford degree and
how she writes all the time. She's on book
number three, you know. I wish you really
were, as she says, lingering between the lines."

She takes three more books with her to hold as
she watches TV. Later, she'll lay her head on one
and finally fall into a gentle slumber where she
is always beautiful and it always 1949.

He waits for her across the hall and lingers
somewhere between the lines where his heart
beats full of Texas oil and Indian Ink.

Tempest in My Teacup

Daddy, the tempest is raging. I know, I know. I live in a tea cup but the billows are tossing high and since you've been gone, no shelter or help is nigh. And that is where it gets tricky.

You made me promise not to pray to you when you were gone, but honestly, I didn't think a little talk could hurt. I am not used to questioning God about anything and normally I don't. But recently I realized my teacup is in the center of a three-ring circus and these are indeed my monkeys and they are knocking my cup over and crashing the entire tea set.

So recently I've been hearing in my head " Carest thou not that we perish? How can thou lie asleep? When each moment so deadly is threatening a grave in this angry deep?" because you lie asleep in your blissful grave while I am going down with my ship. You are up there yucking it up playing 42 and drinking root beer with your old time friends. So I am not really praying, I've wondering why everyone sharing your DNA with me is getting the snot kicked out of them by Father Time.

I have been walking around singing,"Daddy the tempest is raging…" as a joke, at first, and then a little bit like I was mad. But it dawned on me today that I was substituting you for The Master. I realized this is what you were talking about when you told me not to pray to you, but pray to God. Because you were leaving me alone with a tempest in my teacup. Then the craziest thing happened….

I remembered. I remembered you. The only song I remember you directly teaching me, fully teaching the tune along with lyrics. One night we sang it over and over again until we got it right. And it was the first grown-up song I ever learned all the words to and I never forgot those precious words. I wasn't a day over four that late night. Today, I suddenly realized The Master is in my Tempest and no water can swallow the ship where lies the Master of Ocean and Earth and sky.

You left me alone to make room for Jesus in my boat. The tempest can rage all around me if Jesus is hanging out down below serving as the ballast for my ship. The waves can toss, the monkeys can mutiny, but the storm can't have me and I will make safe harbor.

In God's good time. When Jesus decides it's time to join me on deck and give the command for my whole stinking teacup to pipe-down and give it a rest. But until then, I lean into the spray, taste the salt on my lips without fear because Jesus is riding with me. He's just down below taking it easy. And maybe, I too should take it easy trusting Him to come up at the right time and take control of the ship. It's time to let go and let him guide the vessel. I never wanted to be captain anyway.

Peace, Be Still.

That's the deal.

Daddy, you brilliantly tattooed the words of that song on my heart so when life stripped me naked, Master The Tempest Raging was revealed in indelible ink all over my soul.

Where is Jesus when I cannot see him? When I am alone on my sinking ship, where is God? He is down below balancing out things. Keeping this craft from turning over.

Master, the tempest is raging in my little teacup.

Amazing Grace

Amazing Grace

 Amazing Grace…

A daddy comes,

a daddy goes,

Leaving you at the window.

Better that he came

Than if he never did

And chose you

For his precious kid.

The world is cruel

But he was kind

And lives forever

In your heart and mind.

 Daddy stays

 Inside of you

And never leaves

Your heart so true.

See him on the beach

Feel him in the sun

Hold him in your heart

When day is finally done.

Daddy's come,

But never really go

They watch over you

From heaven's window.

He stands there young

Watching for your heart.

Waiting for the day

You'll never have to part.

Hand in hand, you'll walk the surf

Laughing in the wind

Momma waves from up the beach

The day will never end

When Martha walks though Heaven's gate

Beyond the devil's reach

And Daddy waves and calls to her

To join him on the beach.

That is when it all makes sense

When sorrow comes no more

And Daddy's always ever there

On that blessing shore

When Martha finally runs to him

And he will wait no more

To catch her up in his arms

Just like he did before.

Laughter rings down beach

 Joy spreads over his face

As Martha raises her voice to sing

Of God's Amazing Grace.

Daddy went, but Jesus came

And made things right again

Covering us in His precious blood

So we can meet again.

Amazing Grace,

How sweet the sound...

Momma At The Looking Glass

Momma come to the looking glass,
I want your heart to see
Who you have always been
Let's refresh your memory.

Artist, teacher, Mother, friend
You always had a part
In all the happy days
Kept sealed within my heart.

One day you stepped out side
With a sack of corn meal
And turned our whole backyard
Into our a football field

Some one yelled ,"Hey, Coach, think fast!"
Throwing the ball too quick
Your glasses broke in half
And the frames could not be fixed

First I panicked, then I cried
And tried to run away
You called me to come back
"Hey, we have a game to play."

Daddy wanted to whoop my rear
But you'd have none of that
You came back glasses taped
Wearing a Tom Landry hat!

Once the neighbors barn burned down
 I's blameless as could be
You quizzed the firemen
 Preparing to defend me

Dad ran home to see the flames
 Bad kids put the blame on me
You already had my back
 And pled my case so calmly,

Daddy calmed down and kissed my cheek
So glad we were alright
He took us out to eat
And tucked me in bed that night.

The day I flew off the roof
Batman's cape failed on me
You saw me out your window
 And screamed "Oh, my sweet baby!"

I guess we almost killed you
Raising us happy 'n free
You were the best of mothers

To both my siblings and me.

Momma come to the looking glass
See what is in my heart
Of all the best things in life
You are the most precious part.

Crepuscule Skies

A woman child sways beneath the night

Whispering to the Texas moon

Stars fall from an Oxford sky

She strings them round her heart

To go out waltzing

And only dance

With a lad

Named

Life.

Mountain Muses

'The Three Little Pigs" is said to be about building your life so well that nothing can touch you. WRONG. Dead wrong. Nothing could keep death out, and the last house was easiest for the wolf to enter once he thought of the chimney. What makes the story worth telling is that it teaches us about the power of our tribes. During catastrophe, each pig runs for the safety of his brother and seeks the help of his tribe. Death looms reminding them to whom they belong and where to find safety. When the tribe of three brothers reassembles, the power to defeat death is not within the physical walls provided by the richest, smartest brother but within the fellowship's ability to adapt and assist each other in the face of impending doom. They find a solution that not only saves them but nourishes their lives. Alone, they could not out-live death. Together, they out-love it.

I spent my childhood in Arkansas. The state is known as the land of the razorback hog. My tribe formed and originated in the small college town of Searcy, Arkansas. No matter how far I roam, and I do roam, I always find

myself connected to that tribe from that town.
When calamity strikes, or death appears on the
doorstep, it is to those people that I run. I go
back to the people who are my safe space.
When life turns out just right, and the joy of
success is too much for my heart to contain, I
climb into my time machine and click a pen.
And my tribe is always the first to cheer me on.

My heart keeps backing up to my tribe.
No matter how many times I clicked my pen to
move forward, I find myself thinking about
thirty little Arkansas razorbacks running up and
down the mountains, facing The Big Bad Wolf,
and safely returning home to our tribe.

Repelling

I sit down, to set down, on this page, memories in the travel journal of my heart. It usually travels backwards, and sometimes it spirals down the way it does tonight. I am geared-up with ropes, climbing tools, and pen prepared to descend ledge to ledge.

From the top of my memories, the view is clear. I can see where my tribe tumbled years ago to land and settle into each other's lives. The collective pressures and trials of our times compressed and hardened us into the bedrock from which we climb toward the light. If we fall, we always land on each other. When we land, there is enough love to cushion, and in the end, save us.

Cherwell Dreams

Reflections on losing my summer in Oxford due
to the pandemic...

I wish to walk on moon beams
brush stardust from my hair
Reach the magic midnight sky
find diamonds winking there
String them on a silken cord
hang them in my heart.

Dance with fools on Folly's bridge
next to an Oxen cart.
I have waited for these dreams of mine
longer than you can know…
For heaven and earth to align for me
to pack my bags and go.

But COVID came with the breath of death,
grabbed my string of dreams,
And popped the cord and shook the stars,
to tumble in the stream.
I wade into the Cherwell now,
and find my stars again…

I'll string another set of dreams,
to share with you, my friend.

Apple Tree

25

Your brother
Showed me
Where you slept
Under the apple tree.

He pawed 'n cried
Layed down
At your side
Beneath the apple tree

I dug a
A grave
With my love
Beside the apple tree

And layed your
squeaky
Charlie Brown
Aside the apple tree

Now with you he
Lies and
Sweetly rests
Under the apple tree

Rest my lads
Amid
Evening shade
Beneath my apple tree

Sea Worthy

He was a true soul, and Jim taught me that God created me with the ability to weather the storm. I am road worthy. Sea worthy. Lean into the spray and navigate wisely and with confidence.

By the time I knew him, he'd reached that place a man comes to where he knew who he was. He was wild and free like a bear or an eagle and pretty mucn in tune with God that way. He just knew where he was going like that. You never see a bear or a whale or an eagle asking directions. They just walk, or fly, or navigate naturally as God intended and there is no doubt what their habits are or how they will act or what the motivations are. Jim was like that. His life had made him like a rock that the surf crashes against.

Jim had Viking hands. Vikings rowed so much, they developed these huge squared off hands you can only get rowing all your developmental life. I never told him, but I learned that in Viking studies. All those years rowing in wild Alaskan seas had taught him a lot about God and suredness and staying a course and how impossible things can be realized if you lean into the wind and don't give up. He lived that in a way I had never seen any other man do.

 I flew to Juneau the day after Jim died and got off the plane and got in the Jeep and drove toward the Mendenhall. You know how the mountain rises as the road curves out that way? Jim's whole life flashed through my mind being summed up and preaching it's only sermon. For a man of little words and never to preach, he was the wild man of God who just anchored his soul to Christ as naturally as the eagle glides into the horizon and he would no more sink than a whale would drown and not because of who he was but because of Who he belonged to. As summer comes, the Alaskan outdoors will surely feel unbalanced without him, but those of us who search for his face and feel an ache for Jim's companionship must remember that God is in His heaven and all is well. No shadow comes without the dawn lighting the way...

Tu

" Je suis Gassama"

"Merci, Mamoudou!! Merci!"

he walks the Champs Elysee

mothers clutching little red spiders

" C'est Lui!" they whisper

and hold up their precious ones to

adore their hero

the Spiderman

who traveled the desert and crossed the seas

to save a child of Paris.

Macron waits at the palace

but he will take a moment

here

in the streets

to feel the tears

of thousands of fathers

who have opened their hearts

to lay their Paris at his feet

his precious feet

that with mighty hands

scaled the tower

to save every child

of Paris.

Come, children!

Wrap him in our flag

And ask him to say " tu"

For he is our brother.

"Lui, c'est mon frère."

" Bienvenue `a la maison!"

Feast on our love

rest in our hearts

for you are home

Buckaroo

You took my love and my heart
And crushed me beneath your shoe
And wiped what was left there on the mat
And that was the end of you.

But it's not the end of me, Oh no,
I've survived the wind and the rain
I'll gather myself like flower petals
And learn to bloom again.

For the rain has been my friend ,you see,
It wouldn't let me die
It ran in rivets and torrents here
And raised me to the sky

Away from the place before your door
Where once you wiped your feet
It washed me to a safer place
And piled me in a heap.

There's lots here to work with now
And the sun is shining bright
I'll wash my face and fix my hair
And I will be alright.

So watch your step there, Buckaroo
Don't trip on your own life,
Don't let the door hit you in your rear
Because I have left and took my light.

Escape

Take me way
to anywhere
Make me a citizen
 of someday

Now
right now
no delays

 I bought my ticket from a huckster
who left with my past
 and my future
and
trapped me
in the present

A cage
 a dirty cage
uncomfortable and
 not mine

I don't trust today

 So tomorrow
get me out of here

We'll ease out
just before dawn
drift into the sunrise
set sail for someday
sometime
 somewhere.

I feel my time running out.

So quickly,
 as the first rays stream across the dawn
Take me
 Away
to Someday.

What If?

What if I am an idiot?

What if my whole life

Was one big waste

And what if living through Cancer

With a handicap

Was a mistake?

What if all my family

Doesn't really Love me

And it's all fake?

What if time goes on forever?

With foes and not friends

And all forsake

What if Alaska doesn't miss me?

The Shrine isn't real or

No salmon bake

What if everything I loved

Has left me alone?

For pity's sake

Then I'll climb up on Nikki's back!

She knows how it feels

And I need a break

We'll take a trip up to Skagway!

Meet Romeo there

For old time sake.

They left each of us just to die!

None worth a fuss or

Trouble we'd make.

We're a big disappointment now!

We didn't entertain

Shot, starved, and lame

We don't need the old nay-sayers!

It's our turn to live

Let's a fuss make

We'll ride the White Pass to Texas!

I'll turn up the air

Make y'all honey cake.

A wolf- bear lady lives within me

Who deserves from life

What she can make.

Come dance with the Nikki in me

And Romeo too.

Come, and bring cake!

For Audrey: To The Moon and Back

I often say that I love you to the moon and
back. 27 years ago, the moon winked, a star
laughed ever so sweetly,and you were born.

From the first moment you squinted at the lights
in the delivery room,
you have served as the most convincing
evidence that God not only loves us, but that he
actually likes us.

I could not have known how God would fill
and bless my life the way he did pressing it
down and topping it off on July 25, 1992, and
brimming it to over flowing with the gift of you
filling me with more joy than you can imagine.

My favorite phrase became, " Look, Aunt
Mar!" as you showed me a toy, a new dress, or
a favorite dog. And all your life you've supplied
me with reasons to smile and be happy.

When my nights grow a little too dark or my
heart dim, I look around in the atmosphere and
you are out there still shining and twinkling and

winking hope my way. Your laughter always
lifts my heart to the stars. I am so, so lucky to be
within your orbit. I shall always love you to the
moon and back, my dear friend. To the moon
and back

Windows

I sat with my head down looking out the window that over looked the playground and across the street to where the preacher lived. He had one of the brick houses that sat ringed round Harding's little park. My friends had told me who all lived where. I supposed you had to be pretty important to have a house there. I had not played there yet, but some of the children had said there was a little river that ran through it. That you could catch frogs there and climb trees. It was like Central Park in New York City, only it was in the middle of Harding.

I sat in front of that window for what seemed like hours. Finally, a man and a woman emerged from a house that sat on the north side of Harding Park. I had never seen them before, but I knew they had to be his parents. The man had all the brisk movements of a man on a mission and the woman calmly matched her steps to his as he steered her across the street with his arm cupped around her waist. The hem of her skirt flipped as he guided her across the grass, and I remember wondering if it would stain her shoes as she kept pace with him. Half way across, his arm fell from behind her and they grasped hands

with out missing a beat. Without looking. As
they skirted the play ground fence and
disappeared around the back of the school
building, I resolved to go with grace. To take the
horrible verbal scourge I knew was coming
without argument. To spare my father any
further embarrassment. So I sat stock-still and
waited. The sun was almost blinding as it
streaked across the window and lit up the
stairwell. Nothing moved or made a sound.
Death had come. Social and academic death.
Eventually the silence was shattered by the
sound of steps approached from down the hall.
They made the turn toward the lower landing
below the stairs- clipped and hurried. The only
sound they made was that of two pairs of shoes
beating as one and practically flying across the
parkay patterned linoleum. Half way up the
stairs, the footsteps stopped, and I hung my head
as low as it would go. Then, very lightly they
proceeded slowly, almost gently. Like someone
searching for something along the way. My heart
was beating rapidly and it was hard to breathe.
And then some one was saying my name.
Gently, the way my father said my name. But it
wasn't my father and so I didn't look up. I
waited. Then I heard my name again.
" Look at me. Margie, raise your head and look
at me."

I lifted my head and struggled to straighten my neck.

" Open your eyes and look at me."

I opened my eyes and looked directly into the preacher's eyes. Looking back now, I can't say if he was stooped over or he had stooped down, but he had lowered himself to my level.

" Margie, I need to talk to you…"

Oddly enough, he didn't sound like a man who was going to throw me out of school. He didn't sound like a man wielding power. He didn't sound like a man who thought he was better than everyone else. He didn't sound like anything I had imagined. What he sounded like was a man really worried.

"Margie, I want to thank you."

I was shocked by the look in his eye as he stooped there in front of the window and thanked me for stopping his on the play ground- for helping him raise his son. He talked to me like I was an adult. He expressed the concern that he had as a father trying to raise his son to be a good man. He was concerned about what was going to happen if his son was treated with kit-gloves because he was a preacher's son. He was honest and compassionate and I had a "get out of jail free" pass.

Windows changed for me the year the preacher
knelt and spoke with me beneath the window.
Until then, I had been afraid of windows. A
drug addict might climb through one. The Faulk
monster might grab me. A genetically
engineered frog might zap me with his
enormous, sticky tongue and drag me over the
sill and into the night. I was sure only bad
things happened to those who dared linger
around windows.
I changed the morning a red kick ball zinged and
pinged and introduced me to the man who taught
me to look people in the eye and watch
hopefully out the window

Fancy Crystal

I drink coke and fruit juice from famous Irish
crystal just to prove I am strong, and maybe, just
maybe, if I am honest, to spit in your face. Oh,
and I own a lot of it. I let anyone drink out of it
especially the dogs. I buy it for myself, my
doctor, for friends and everyone who never even
heard your name. I use the crystal every day.   I
suppose because you said I was a nigger not
worthy of touching it.

"Do you know how much this cost? You fucking
nigger?"

Why yes, yes, I do and sometimes I throw some
away because I can. Just like I threw you away
once I was brave enough to run.

The places your proved you were a man still hurt
me. I suppose they always will. A cautionary
tale to never let a man hurt me again. I thought
it all would stop hurting by now. I still have an
irrational fear of leather belts and whiskey
bottles.

I have tried to remember you when were kind
and funny and gentle. They say you have to
forgive, but I get nothing. There is nothing. The
fellow who would protect me all my life is a
blank. You are a total blank. No size. No shape.
No face. I can't dial in anyone but the monster.
If I stop to remember the monster, I can see that
face, hear that voice, and remember the words
that tore me to pieces like an eagles talons. And
running and dodging and freezing like a
frightened rabbit because you were a man and I
was a nigger. And that was that.

One frightening night, I stopped being
humiliated and ashamed and I left you. Granted,
it was more like an emergency evacuation with
cops at intersections and one escorting me safely
out of town. I left you and your exploitation and
manipulation. It was a hard way to grow up, but
I made it.

It was a long time ago and I can't remember
you especially when I drink from my fancy
crystal.

Our Gomer

She weeps alone
with a magazine
as her angry bazooki
screams for doxycycline.

Who will take her ice
from McD's or Sonic?
When your Bazooki's on fire,
ice is a tonic.

She's not asking much,
just respite from pain,
please turn down
the airconditioner again.

She would,if she could ,
strip naked in the rain,
run barebrested through the streets
to keep from going insane.

She feels like Gomer,
at the end of the day,
worn out and tired
of being on display

LIke an old over head projector
whose bulb is on fire
She's sick of being hot and
Our sanctimonious ire.

Lye naked dear lady,
and do not dismay
for medicine and ice
are coming your way.

Taunt not our dear Gomer,
for being on display,
less your bazooki catch a blaze
in this very same way.

For heat curses us all
in our own day,
and soon your jiggly bits
may be burning away.

Taunt not our dear Gomer.

Jesus Loves Me

There must be a devil

You don't seem to see

Because you almost

Had me convinced

God doesn't love me.

But I know Jesus Loves Me

I spend lots of time with him

And speak often with His Father

He won't let me

Live in fear again.

Go on and live your life superior

Abandon me with all this mess

Walk with your head held high

Above a struggling heart

Amid a puffed up chest.

To the victor goes the spoils

Losers are stuck with all the rot

That's fine impressive theory

But there is something

you've forgot.

I know Jesus Loves Me

I sang it as a kid

You can betray

and abandon me

But Jesus never did.

So you come round here bragging

Show me all that's shiny and new

Call me nigger

Call me trash

I'll practice forgiveness on you.

For I am old and tired

I have done what I can do

And though you have thrown me

To the wolves

I never gave up on you.

I know Jesus loves me

That ought to be enough

When trouble comes to my door

When seas turn

Dark and rough.

I know there is a devil

'Cause he's at us once again

Your sea's growIng mighty rough

Let me help you

You my old friend.

 Cause I know Jesus loves Me

The Price We Pay

Money buys a lot of things...

Take all your new cars

Go on a cruise

Enjoy the ocean

Float in your pool

Hire some one

 to take care of you

Go to the ballgame

The concerts

The mall

The winery

Go do it all

Because that

 is what

money buys

And truck loads

of betrayal

Run around town

Fly to Nome

Evade your taxes

Buy another home

Shop 'til you drop

Steal a car

You don't need

When you could

Buy one and

Not steal it

From me.

Don't forget

Sunday school

Fund raise

 and defame

Enjoy the convention

Drop name

 after name

Because that

Is what

Money buys

And a bag full of betrayal.

Money pays

For a lot of

Betrayal

And abandonment

And lies

And defamation

And alienation

And disgrace

And shame.

Shame

Shame

Shame

Shame

Shame.

Money buys

A lot of

Shame.

You can wear it

Like a new hat

To my funeral

Tell everyone

Dumb enough

to listen

How valiant

 you are

How helpful

you've been

About good times

We supposedly had

Way back when

I was loyal

I was true

Doing all

those things

I did for you

Money buys a lot of things…

Like

When I was school age, all that mattered was who loved you. We said the word "like," but we really meant "love." Like means someone will share their cookies and skip rope with you. They'll push you in the swing so you can fly high. When I got into the double digits, I'd get asked to the dance or find a red valentine in my locker. So "like" was a big deal, and if I was liked enough, I'd eventually be loved, and in my little kids' heart, that meant I'd never be alone. And that was pretty well how it worked until I grew up and refuse to admit that who didn't love me mattered, and I was going to wind up alone without any cookies or valentines and searching for a face in the crowd to like me. I finally came to realize that what I needed to stop throwing my love around stylishly and start asking myself who I could find true "like" with. Who did I honestly want to share my cookies and push my swing?

These questions whispered to me from songs on the radio and from lines in movie scripts, but I then told myself it didn't matter because I was grown up. That is, until it was time for a high school reunion. Or homecoming. Or someone's name popped up on a friend request. And then, there was a funeral. When it's time to bury someone, you realize the little kid questions of like and love are what it all boils down to. Every time we bury someone we love, we come to them with only our heart in our hands. One last red valentine, if you will.

When my first grade school seatmate, Alan, passed away. We made the journey back home, again, and helped his momma give him back to God. The red clay from Alan's grave stained my sky-blue Uggs in a big blob of red like a red valentine. I never had it cleaned away. When I doubt who I am, I drag them out, put them on, look down and remember the days of like.

www.ingramcontent.com/pod-product-compliance
Lightning Source LLC
La Vergne TN
LVHW051229200726
843510LV00011B/1532